The Wholesaler's Guide To Closing Real Estate Deals

Other books by Kevin Sayles:

Probate Real Estate Sales 101: A Guide For Real Estate Agents And Investors is available on Amazon.

More coming soon! Stay tuned at www.KevinSayles.com.

The Wholesaler's Guide To Closing Real Estate Deals

(And How Agents Can Structure Deals For Their Investors)

Kevin Sayles

ISBN-13: 9781792881367

DISCLAIMER

The purpose of this material is to help investors and real estate professionals understand the various ways of closing wholesale transactions. Neither the publisher nor author is engaged in providing advice of any type, especially financial, legal and tax advice. The information contained herein is considered accurate and was written based on the expertise of the author, a 20-plus year veteran in the industry. However, the information contained herein is not guaranteed. If legal, tax or other advice is required, desired, or necessary, consult an appropriate, competent professional. Your results may vary from the examples, scenarios, and case studies presented. Names have been changed to protect confidentiality.

Furthermore, the author and publisher do not guarantee or warranty that any tips, techniques, suggestions, strategies, or ideas will apply to every situation. In real estate in general, every situation is different and requires a different solution. Any place within this material where another organization, company or website is mentioned as a source of further information does not constitute an endorsement of such entity.

The reader acknowledges that some entities referenced within this material may be businesses affiliated with the author and/or publisher.

This material was written based on an understanding of real estate closing procedures in the state of California. Many other states have similar rules and procedures, but there can be wide variance state by state. In fact, even within California, there may be procedural differences county by county. Check with your local governing body, legal and tax advisors to ensure you are following local guidelines.

CONTENTS

ACKNOWLEDGMENTS

I want to thank God for my life, my abundance and the things that I have learned over my career and been able to share in this book. I am thankful for my family. Thank you to my 4 boys for being the brightest joy in my life. Thank you to my parents for raising me to be a man. And most of all thank you to my wonderful wife...Darla, my dreamgirl.

PREFACE

Numerous reality house-flipping shows and house-flipping workshops introduce the average person to making money in real estate. When I was growing up, it was late night infomercials with real estate gurus selling programs to teach you how to invest in real estate. Some of those gurus ended up with class action lawsuits and/or criminal records. I am glad that mainstream TV and legitimate investors have been able to spread the knowledge of how people can make a great living or augment their current financial situation through real estate investing.

I learned about real estate investing from a few unsuspecting clients at the bank where I worked. They didn't know it (or maybe they did), but they mentored me. One in particular taught me the power of leverage. Real estate is an investment that has unmatched leverage to help you make money. Another taught me the power of cash flow. This knowledge came to me by observing them in their transactions and them spending a little time to teach me a few concepts.

Since 1993 my career has taught me the ins

and outs of real estate. My first six years in banking got me started and made me interested in investing in real estate. The last 20+ years working for closing agents have given me laser-scoped precision in closing deals in challenging situations. It is this information that I share with you in this book.

This material started out as an informational flyer that I shared with real estate agents and investors. There were "11 Different Ways To Close A Double Escrow". This quickly grew to 15 ways as different situations presented themselves. The term "Double Escrow" became taboo (at least in California), caused lawsuits and was followed by growth of the term "wholesaling" (see ch. 15 for more details). Therefore, this material morphed into what it is today.

Now, with 20+ ways for a wholesaler to make money in this business…we have this book. It is written from my heart and mind in a way that anyone can understand. I hope you enjoy reading it and that it helps you make tens of thousands of dollars in your real estate career!

INTRODUCTION

The Wholesaler's Guide To Closing Real Estate Deals

Wholesale

In today's real estate market, wholesaling is generally defined as **selling a property to an investor at a price that is lower than the current market price of a property in good condition.** The purpose of doing so is to leave profit in the property so that the investor can rehab the property and sell it to an end user at fair market value. The current market price of a property in good condition is called the **After Repair Value or ARV.**

Wholesaling is different from retail selling. "Retailing" a property which would be **to sell the property to a homeowner (end user) who plans to live in it or use it as a rental property** and is what normal homeowners do when they sell the home they live in.

Wholesaling is often the way individuals start their real estate investing career as it requires little or no money to begin. Additionally, wholesale transactions typically close quickly. Therefore, they are a fast path to profits.

A-B-C

Every wholesale deal starts out the same way. Party A (the seller) is motivated to sell a property. Party B (you, the wholesaler) negotiates a price with Party A. Party C (the "end buyer" found by Party B) desires to buy the property for a price higher than the price negotiated between A and B. Party B wishes to profit by making the difference between the price negotiated with A and the price C is willing to pay.

At times when you find yourself in this beautiful situation, there can be challenges to closing the deals. This usually is because the property is in some sort of distress. Examples of distress that you find on a property are:

- delinquent taxes

- personal liens of the seller

- mortgage delinquency

- foreclose (bank owned property)

- short sale

- deceased owner (probate or trust sale)

- city or county liens against the property

- deferred maintenance

- sub-par condition of the property

- etc.

The challenges that are created by each different type of distress vary widely. It is for this reason that this book has been written.

Structure

Where these transactions can become a little muddy is how B structures this transaction in order to profit. How important is this? Well, there are many failed investors, money losers and even folks that are now wearing orange jumpsuits or striped outfits that will tell you...**how you structure the transaction is the most important part!**

What is the big deal about how you structure the transaction? Why all the fuss? Structuring the transaction is what ensures that you *legally* close the sale. The structuring of the transaction determines how the wholesaler is to be paid. The transaction is structured based on the goals of the parties (A, B, and C), who the other interested parties are (i.e. a short sale lender, an REO bank, if institutional lenders are involved, if the property is being taken subject to encumbrances) and liens.

The details of the transaction can vary dramatically. How the deal is structured will depend on the details of the scenario and the type of sale. For example, the purchase of an REO property (bank owned) is different than a property that is a pre-foreclosure. A short sale is different from a standard equity sale, which is different from a probate. What if the seller does not allow an assignable contract? What if the seller places deed restrictions (institutional sellers will at times place restrictions such as: one cannot sell the property for 20% more than the current sales price for 90 days)? There are several moving parts and variables which make up the scenario. Typically, each scenario is different.

For this reason, there are many solutions. The solutions provided in this material should be used in specific situations. Some solutions will not work in all cases. At times, one can employ more than one of these solutions on the same transaction. An investor should choose the solution that makes the most sense in their particular scenario. It is also recommended that buyer, seller and wholesaler seek both legal counsel and tax advice from appropriate professionals.

Before we dive in…note that most of these methods of closing transactions cannot be accomplished without the assistance of skilled professionals. Be sure that you have the correct team in place! Your closing agent, escrow officer, title company, legal counsel, tax advisors and real estate advisors must know what they are doing.

The #1 Tip For Newbies When Getting Started (and experienced investors as well)

You decide to get into real estate investing. You have seen enough house flipping TV programs that you realize that you can do it too! You go to a few seminars, attend some real estate investment meetings and learn the basics. Now you start looking for distressed property. Finally, after putting in the work, you find your first deal. Congratulations!!

Now here is what I want you to always remember: Protect your investment! Of course this means protect your money but it also means protect your time, your resources, your team, etc. It is very easy to get into a deal, put up money as an earnest money deposit or for an option and not take the proper steps to protect your investment.

Remember, homeowners (sellers), buyers, other investors and real estate agents can make mistakes or be fraudsters. People make commitments that they do not keep. If your money is relying on a commitment rather than something more solid...beware.

One way to protect yourself is to follow the big money. For instance, if you are funding your money for a loan, financing on a property or even just your down payment funds, make sure you are obtaining title insurance. A bank would not fund a loan for $20,000 without requiring title insurance, so why shouldn't you obtain it to insure your $20,000 down payment? Follow the big money (institutional money) and use the safety precautions that they use.

Another way to protect your investment is to do your transaction as similar to other "normal" transactions as possible. For instance, buy the property with a normal contract, closing services and escrow period whenever possible. This gives sellers less ability to imagine they are being taken advantage of and protects you against lawsuits.

Structuring Your Wholesale Transactions

The following pages describe methods of structuring your wholesale transaction and are in no specific order.

1. Agreements for Fees Outside of Escrow

What happens outside of escrow stays outside of escrow! It is not anyone else's business. I have seen everything from money given to the seller… to money given to the wholesaler outside of escrow. Be very careful making side arrangements as this can be very tricky. First of all, you have to trust that you will be paid (Rule #1 of real estate investing: never trust anyone). Second, in some states, in some situations and depending on credentials of parties involved (for example if one party is a real estate licensee) it may be illegal.

👍 **Benefits:** Very easy to set up.

👎 **Drawbacks:** Possibly illegal. Not guaranteed. Similar to a handshake deal which is not recommended. You must figure out a way to secure your fee.

🎯 **Potential Uses:** When dealing with family members or well-trusted individuals.

2. Buy the Property in an Entity

The ownership of the entity can be sold, changed or transferred in order to accomplish your desired result. Just like selling a house, car or any other asset, one can sell an entity that they own. For example, Party B owns Corporation X. Party B negotiates the sale of a house from Party A to Corporation X. Corporation X then owns a home that was purchased from Party A. Party B has lined up a buyer named Party C. Party B then sells the corporation to Party C. The property remains in the name of Corporation X, however, the ownership of the corporation has changed.

Typically, with this type of scenario, investors use Limited Liability Companies or Corporations.

👍 **Benefits:** No change in ownership of the property when C takes over. Anonymity of party C.

👎 **Drawbacks:** There may be significant paperwork for the change of ownership of the entity. The assistance of legal counsel and tax professionals is almost absolutely necessary in order to sell the corporation properly. It is risky for Party C as they assume the liability and debts of the corporation. Property tax re-assessments may be triggered. Title insurance coverage may be voided/changed as a result of change in ownership of the entity.

Potential Uses: When the A-B end of the transaction comes with deed restrictions or resale restrictions. When preventing a change in ownership from party B to C is required.

3. Placing a Loan or Mortgage on the Property

This method was widely used when Double Escrows became taboo. The deed of trust can be used to secure the monetary interest of an investor, partner, wholesaler or hard money lender. For example, A is selling directly to C (as a result of B putting together the deal). As part of C's financing, a loan to B is being placed on the property at the close of the sale from A to C. Just as C can owe money to a bank, C can also owe money to B. Typically, the closing agent prepares the loan documents for the loan.

Real Scenario: *A client of mine (B) was in a situation where the contract was set up between A and C. The closing agent would not handle an assignment fee and they were too far along in the transaction to have to cancel the transaction with that closing agent and start all over with another. B wanted to ensure that the money they were owed was part of the deal, in writing and secured for payment later. The best solution was to put the money that was owed to B (in this case $10,000) as a loan against the property in 2nd lien position behind the purchase money loan.*

This made all parties happy and B was paid out upon the sale of the property with interest!

In another scenario, B was putting up the down payment money for the sale of the property from A to C. C was the original person that found the property and A was an REO bank. The bank would not allow assignment of the contract, nor adding another person or entity to the contract. B and C decided to put a 2nd mortgage on the property to secure B's money. After closing the sale (from A to C), C then added B onto the title of the property in the correct proportional interest and B removed the loan from the property.

In this second scenario, B was a newer investor and was planning to give their money to partner on the deal without any security. This would have been one of those rookie mistakes that I addressed in the beginning.

👍 **Benefits:** Secured by the property. May charge interest on the profit until paid (the profit to the wholesaler structured in the deal is the principal loan balance). May be used to create a passive income stream (loan payments).

👎 **Drawbacks:** If C is obtaining financing to purchase the property, B's loan will be in a subordinate lien position (a 2nd or 3rd mortgage) which is much more risky. This also requires a level of trust between B and C. Remember, C could have a change of heart and close the transaction with all cash and cut you out. Know your closing agents. You must wait to be paid off. Lack of control (it is someone else's property, the note holder has little control over the property or its owners). Foreclosure of the loan is the only recourse if things go wrong.

Potential Uses: Non-assignable contracts (C's money is used to purchase the property by B who is the wholesaler and buyer on the contract). After the close of escrow, B transfers the property to C. Potentially in situations with deed restrictions. Also, see the scenarios above.

4. Placing a Loan or Mortgage on the Property Then Foreclosing on the Loan

This method requires time, and pre-planning. Essentially, a loan is placed on the property by the party that wishes to obtain ownership, person X. That loan is then foreclosed. Person X becomes the owner once the foreclosure has occurred.*

👍 **Benefits:** Same as #3. One additional benefit is that the foreclosure may wipe out certain liens/encumbrances that may be on the property. This may be most beneficial if you are able to buy a lien or loan that is already against the property in a more senior lien position. In other words, purchasing a lien or loan that was recorded against the property years ago allows you to wipe out all the loans/liens that are recorded after the lien that you purchase and foreclose upon. Typically, foreclosures will wipe out liens that are recorded after the loan is recorded against the property. There are some exceptions so seek proper legal advice.

👎 **Drawbacks:** Same as #3. Foreclosure is a lengthy process in any state. In non-judicial foreclosure states, the process is typically faster and does not require court involvement. Either way, this is a long-term way of acquiring a property. Foreclosure is also a costly process and requires proper advice from professionals. Additionally, the owner of the property can delay the foreclosure by filing bankruptcy. Some homeowners are very skilled at delaying foreclosures. Beware! Seek legal advice!!

*Loss of control—in many states, the foreclosure process includes an auction to the highest bidder. There is no guarantee that the property will be coming back to the individual that places the loan. However, if someone else buys it at the foreclosure auction, at least the person will receive their money back plus costs of foreclosure (as allowed by the loan documents and/or state laws).

🎯 **Potential Uses:** Typically only favorable when an impending lien is coming and one wants to secure their interest prior to that lien appearing or when purchasing a lien that is already secured against the property. Not typically recommended in judicial foreclosure states. Follow the rules for placing loans and foreclosing in your area!

5. Assign the Contract in a Separate Escrow

The right to buy a property can be sold/assigned just as any physical item can be sold. In this method of wholesaling, the sale of the contractual right to buy a property is handled in a separate escrow.

For example, A enters an assignable contract to sell the property to B. There is an escrow opened for the **sale of the property** from A to B, let's call it Escrow 1. B Sells the right to that contract/escrow to C. There is an escrow opened for the sale of the **right to the A-B contract**, in which B is the seller and C is the buyer, let's call this one Escrow 2. The amount of Escrow 2 is the amount of the wholesaler's fee plus or minus costs. C places the assignment fee in Escrow 2 before the contract is assigned in Escrow 1. Escrow 2 is closed in conjunction with and continent upon Escrow 1. Escrow 1 closes from Seller A to buyer C (because B assigned their right to buy the property to C). Escrow 2 closes with C's payment for the assignment to B.

This is one of the most flexible ways to close assignments. It is legal in almost all situations. It gives B privacy over the amount of the assignment fee. It gives B and C control over when deposits are made, when the A-B contract is assigned in escrow, and control and security over when money is transferred to B.

Control is crucially important. Lack of it is how wholesalers get burned. C will typically want the payment to B to be made only upon closure of the assigned sale from A to C. That is the plan and what is scheduled. However, what happens if the seller has some problem and cannot close the sale to C? What if the property is foreclosed upon by the bank before the sale can be consummated? What if there is a water leak, vandalism, break-ins, that create additional damage? What if a natural disaster causes damage to the house before the close of escrow from A to C. If C has already given B the money for the assignment and there is some closing problem, C would be out of luck. Have you ever given someone $10,000 then tried to get it back?

Now let's look at this from B's perspective. If C has not put the money somewhere out of their own control, what guarantee does B have of being paid? As party B, do you assign the contract before being paid? Or do you wait until your money is secured by your 3rd party closing agent before you sign? Assigning the contract through a separate escrow gives you control of these types of issues.

👍 **Benefits:** Control and security over the assignment fee. Privacy of assignment fees. It is very favorable in terms of the legality of wholesaling a property.

👎 **Drawbacks:** Small additional cost for the second escrow. Some escrow companies may not handle the escrow for the assignment (Escrow 2). Can only be used with assignable contracts.

🎯 **Potential Uses:** Can be used in almost all situations with assignable contracts. Is favorable in short sales. This is the preferred method in almost all situations.

5. (a) An assignment fee on an assignable contract. At the original writing of this book, #5 was the method that we were often seeing used to close transactions (after the mortgage meltdown of 2008). This

has now been updated. In today's market, many escrows are more familiar with wholesalers and wholesale fees (thanks to the growing popularity of wholesaling). Therefore, today method #5 has been simplified into method #5(a), where there is only one escrow based on an assignable contract. Out of that escrow, an assignment fee is paid to party B by party C. This is a simpler more streamlined process. It has the same potential uses, benefits and drawbacks as #5.

Party B should make sure that their assignment fee (from C) is in escrow prior to assigning the contract.

Many investors use #5(a) as the default method for wholesaling and only use other methods only when this cannot be employed.

6. Net Listing

This is one of the simplest and easiest ways to secure profits. This method is for real estate agents or brokers. Probably not favorable for a standard single family residence or 1-4 unit owner occupied properties unless they are in really poor condition. However, this is very good for business dealings, challenging or extremely distressed properties, or when the seller is an investor or entity.

Essentially, a net listing is a real estate listing for sale with an agent/broker in which the seller wants a net amount and the agent/broker receives the remainder of the sales price as their profit. For example, seller indicates they want $100k for the home and whatever the agent sells it for over that price is what they keep as commission. It works best when the seller leaves a little meat on the bone and puts a short time deadline on the listing.

One of the main advantages of this strategy is that the seller entices the agent with a greater potential for payout than a normal listing. Imagine, in the example above, if the agent sells it for $120k, they keep the $20k above what the seller wanted for the property. This is an extremely smart strategy when the seller knows that the agent has many investor or buyer contacts and wants to create an additional incentive, and wants to incentivize a quick sale.

If the agent is the wholesaler, the commission becomes the wholesale fee. If the agent is hired by the wholesaler (party B), then wholesale fee is added to the seller's net price to create the net listing amount (i.e. seller's price $100k + $5k wholesaler's fee = net listing at $105k [agent gets amount of sale above $105k as commission]).

Real Scenario: *Through a very interesting probate case, I acquired a property for $55,000. The property was in a very rough gang neighborhood. The property was in poor condition with an elderly woman living in the mold ridden home. This was not long after the mortgage meltdown of 2008 and I did not want to be stuck holding onto this property. My goal was to turn a profit quickly and get out!*

I listed the property with an agent that I knew had very strong connections with house flippers. I knew that they were accustomed to working some of the roughest neighborhoods. I wanted to make $20,000 profit and figured there would be about $2,000 in closing costs. I *did a net listing for $77,000. I figured the property would sell probably somewhere around $85,000 and since normal "pre-mortgage meltdown" commissions where about $10,000, I knew this would be a nice incentive for the agent to sell the home (and make what he used to make when doing so). He sold the property almost immediately for $87,000 and we closed within a few weeks.*

👍 **Benefits:** Creates huge desire in the agents (listing and selling agents if they share the commission) to sell the property.

👎 **Drawbacks:** Seller must have a net amount they require from the property that is below the market value.

🎯 **Potential Uses:** The best use is when the seller does not believe that the market will easily deliver a buyer and/or wants to create an incentive for a fast sale.

7. Close with Cash or Hard Money

This may sound so simple that you wonder…why is this even included? At times, wholesalers and investors are so wound up in the distress of a property or challenges of a situation that they fail to see the simple solution. Close the transaction with cash or a hard money loan (which are readily available in the market today). Then handle the remaining problems, take out permanent financing and/or clean up whatever mess is left after you own the property.

This technique has created a new term in real estate: "Wholetailing" or is it spelled "Wholetaling"…dunno! Essentially, Wholetaling is similar to wholesaling a home, except that party B actually closes the transaction from A to B. Then party B re-sells the property to party C for profit, immediately after closing the first escrow (at least that is the goal and intention). The Real Scenario in #6 is also an example of Wholetaling.

👍 **Benefits:** Simple and straight forward. This method can relieve the time pressure that is often involved in some types of distressed property. It can also allow the buyer to negotiate deeper discounts if there are property issues/risks that are being resolved after the closing of the sale.

👎 **Drawbacks:** Many wholesalers don't have the money to close.

🎯**Potential Uses:** Unlimited.

8. Demand in Escrow

Escrow/closing agents disburse funds from escrow based on demands (payoff statements) that are part of the escrow. If there is a demand for payment in the escrow that is agreed upon by the seller, the escrow will pay it. Therein lies the difficulty with this solution…*agreement from the seller.* Depending on the structure and restrictions of the transaction, a demand in escrow may be the way to go. The sales price can be adjusted to cover the assignment fee if necessary.

👍 **Benefits:** Simple and secure once the seller agrees and approves the demand.

👎 **Drawbacks:** Requires agreement from the seller.

🎯 **Potential Uses:** When the assignment fee is small (or seller doesn't care) and seller is agreeable. This can also be useful when there are assignment restrictions, a non-assignable contract or a non-cooperative party C.

9. Overfund and Buyer Demand in Escrow

This is very similar to #8. The difference here is that the buyer overfunds the escrow by the amount of the assignment fee. Whenever the buyer's side of the escrow has more money than is necessary to close the transaction, escrow gives a refund to the buyer. In this case, there will be an escrow instruction drawn up to issue a refund in the amount of $XX.XX to John Doe (the wholesaler). The seller does not see the buyer's side of the closing statement, therefore, some level of privacy of the assignment fee is maintained. However, if the disbursement is shown on the buyer's side of the closing statement, privacy is not guaranteed.

👍 **Benefits:** Just another way to achieve the same result, especially when other methods won't work. Secures the wholesale fee and allows for privacy.

👎 **Drawbacks:** Some closing agents/escrow companies may not be willing to do this.

Potential Uses: Another alternative to other methods.

10. Land Trust

Land trusts can be very tricky entities! Many title companies and closing agents in California won't even touch land trusts because some of them are not properly set up. Some other states may not have problems with land trusts. Before utilizing a land trust, run it past your closing agent and title company to make sure you will not have any issues. Be cautious of information about land trusts that are used in states other than where you are purchasing the property…rules and customary guidelines may vary state to state.

There are many different benefits to land trusts and one should thoroughly research them with an appropriate attorney and tax advisor to determine if it is the right entity for their situation. Typically when dealing with wholesaling, people employ land trusts because they can change the trustee and/or beneficiary whenever they see fit. Essentially making this similar to closing in an entity (#2).

👍 **Benefits:** Potentially less ongoing fees than other entities. For instance, in California, trusts are not mandated to pay an annual tax that other entities pay.

👎 **Drawbacks:** Not always permitted. Can be costly to set up properly. May draw skepticism from closing agents.

🎯 **Potential Uses:** When the A-B end of the transaction comes with deed restrictions, resale restrictions or assignment limitations. When preventing a change in ownership from party B to C is required.

11. Flip Traditional (make the money and do the work)

Sometimes the deal is such a good deal that you will just buy the property, do the rehab and sell it for profit yourself! That is normally the ultimate goal!

👍 **Benefits:** Can mean a bigger pay day!

👎 **Drawbacks:** Holding time (waiting for return on investment and hoping the market doesn't turn for the negative in the middle of your project), cost of money, potential issues that come up and cut into your profit, ARV not what you thought it would be.

🎯 **Potential Uses:** ANYTIME.

12. The "Skinny Flip"

Buy the property. Do minimal work (less than $5,000 worth for example) sell to end user at a discount or to another investor. In some markets across the U.S., the inventory of homes for sale is far below the demand. This shortage of inventory creates a unique opportunity for investors. This scenario will illustrate:

A 3 Bd 1 Ba house can be purchased by an investor for $300k with an ARV of approximately $430k in tip top shape. Sounds like a great way to make a nice payday. However, in order to obtain $430k, the house requires a full rehab: New kitchen including reconfiguring the floor plan, new bathroom, plus adding a little square footage and a bathroom to make a real master suite. The finished product will be a 3 Bd 2 Ba home that will command $430k. This process will take 3-4 months if you are really fast and have no problems that pop up (the house was built in the early 1900s, so there will likely be things that pop up!). Assuming the rehab runs about $50-60k, it leaves about $70 in profit. When you consider that *carrying costs, the cost of financing, sales costs, taxes, insurance, risks of a vacant home, etc. will eat into this profit a bit more, the deal does not look as sweet. The investor will probably be left with $35-50k or less in profit after about 6 months.*

With the "Skinny Flip", an investor purchased the property and cleaned it up for another buyer to make their own. This home required trash out (to clear out the junk yard that had landed in the back yard), cutting the 2-foot tall grass, an interior paint job, tearing out the old ratty carpet, cleaning the wood floors (not re-finishing) and deep cleaning the whole house. This all cost about $5,000. Afterwards the property was in condition to market to an investor as a flip or an end user who has not been able to compete with the ultra competitive market in the area.

Via the skinny flip the property brought a price of $360k and was in escrow in 3 weeks! Net profit approx. $38k

This method is especially good for Agents. They are able to generate commission on the acquisition and the sale and therefore dramatically increase their profit and number of transactions! This method works in competitive real estate markets with a shortage of housing inventory.

👍 **Benefits:** Less risk than a regular flip. The risks of the market changing, break-ins and vandalism, financing costs, taxes, insurance, etc. are all minimized by the short time period the property is held. Profit is often not much less than a rehab and flip. EXTREMELY beneficial for real estate agents as they generate commissions on the acquisition and the sale.

👎 **Drawbacks:** Less profit than a flip. Depends on the scenario, the investor's stomach for risk and their skill with rehabbing.

🎯 **Potential Uses:** Situations where the profit is not much less than a full rehab given the time and how extensive the rehab will be. Run the numbers to see if a skinny flip is a desirable exit strategy.

13. Cash for Deed

This method of obtaining a property is not used much anymore because of changes in laws that make it risky. There was a time when an extremely distressed homeowner would quitclaim deed their property to an investor for fast cash. You would just find the right seller and give them $50k, $25k or sometimes even $10k and "the property is yours!" In today's legal environment, this method can open up a legal Pandora's box!

First and foremost, the investor may lose the protections under the law that come with being a bona fide purchaser. The full understanding of what this would mean would have to come from an attorney. Generally speaking, it is best to complete a regular sale transaction with escrow and title insurance, with regular time periods, agreements and contracts. Do not underestimate the value of being a bona fide purchaser when it comes to claiming title to a property.

In California, Civil Code 1695 has made it illegal for transactions like this to be done the way many investors used to do them. Any investor that is marketing to property owners that are in default should read, know and understand this civil code. Violation of this law may create a 2-year period that the seller can rescind the transaction. Obtain legal advice to ensure compliance with this code. Check for laws related to investors buying distressed properties in your area.

There are other title related issues that arise with this type of transaction. There may be liens of the seller that are attached to the property that won't be discovered until a title company runs its reports, future requests from title insurance companies for uninsured deed affidavits, and other issues.

The risks of these types of transactions have made them all but obsolete in many real estate markets. Check for the laws in your area.

👍 **Benefits:** Fast.

👎 **Drawbacks:** Laws restrict the use of this method. Risky at best when not closing through title and escrow or closing agent.

🎯 **Potential Uses:** Only as a last resort in situations where legal.

14. Joint Ventures

These can solve a myriad of issues in structuring a transaction and can be used in many different ways. Essentially, a joint venture is where two parties come and do the deal together.

Equity Share JV. In this type of deal, the owner of the property (or it could be the wholesaler) goes in on the transaction with the investor. The equity that is built through the rehab and improvement process is shared by the two parties. In some cases, a seller may have the desire to improve the property to sell it for its maximum value however, they do not have the money to do so. Investors can join in with the seller, finance the rehab and share the profits.

Be cautious with Equity Share JVs and be sure everything is in writing. When doing a JV with the homeowner, it is less risky when the owner does not live in the property. If the owner lives in the property, be very cautious.

Joint Purchase followed by Quitclaim Deed. This is a solution that is used in scenarios where there is no way to assign the contract but another buyer can be added to the purchase.

Real Scenario: *Recently I completed a file this way where HUD was the seller and they would not allow a change of buyer, but would allow another party to be added to the purchase. The other party (let's call them C) was added so that B and C purchased the property together. C was the financier and provided all the money for closing the transaction. After the close of escrow when the deed restriction expired, B received their wholesaling fee and the property was deeded over to C solely.*

Lender JV. Some lenders will do joint ventures with the investor. Typically the lender will provide the lion's share of the financing for the project (or all of the financing) for a cut of the profits. Do plenty of due diligence in these types of transactions. The equity share and lending fees can eat up profits very quickly.

👍 **Benefits:** May be able to help you achieve a higher profit than wholesaling the deal and with little or no additional expense. This method helps put money in another person's pocket as well.

Drawbacks: Make sure you have a good JV partner. Deals can go south quickly when there are numerous parties involved.

Potential Uses: Infinite possibilities. Desirable when the buyer cannot be changed.

15. Double Escrow

The traditional double escrow is pretty much a dinosaur these days. A true double escrow is where there is a contract between A and B and another contract between B and C. B uses the funds from the escrow with C to close the escrow with A. Therefore, B buys the property and sells it at the same time without putting the funds into escrow (except whatever deposit they have on the A-B escrow). This opens up Pandora's box of difficulties as you can probably imagine.

Some closing agents require all parties to be aware of both transactions. If C is buying with a loan, their lender must give written approval to use their funds to close another escrow. With short sales, this is extremely problematic and nearly impossible. In some states, this may be illegal. Just mentioning "double escrow" makes many closing agents cringe.

As mentioned previously, the double escrow is like a dinosaur…extinct! Many of the methods described in this book were developed out of finding a solution that would work when the double escrow would not.

Note: In many states, there may be no issue at all with the double escrow as described here. For California it is not recommended. The closing agents don't like them and the courts don't like them! If you are a real estate agent, you should definitely avoid them because of your fiduciary and ethical responsibility to obtain the best price for the seller.

The reason Double Escrows don't work in California like they may in other states is twofold:

1. California is the most litigious state in the Union! The deal always looks and sounds good when you are helping the seller resolve whatever the situation is…and before they receive their money! However…after you have spent the time and energy to flip it and make $150k and the seller feels *they* should have made that money…or after the seller's nephew is in their ear about how you ripped them off…or after the seller wakes up 2 months later when they have spent all the money they received…or when they find that you listed or sold it

for a profit and they get jealous…etc…then the lawsuit ensues. The courts don't like to hear that you, the investor, made money "*off the back of the poor hardworking seller who trusted you*". I have witnessed countless lawsuits that would have been avoided just by structuring the transaction the right way!

2. In California document recording timing matters. Here in California, a real estate closing happens this way:

   I. The lender funds to the title company (for cash purchases, the money is wired to the escrow or title company).

   II. The transaction is set up for recording (at the county recorder's office) and closing the next day. *Some counties do same day recordings, but not all counties and timing of funding matters.*

   III. The transaction records the next day, then the file is balanced and disbursed. Seller, wholesaler, agents, etc. receive their money after this closing/disbursement day.

As you can see from this process

recording/closing happens one day to the next. When there is an A-B transaction (with no money) and a B-C transaction that is supposed to pay off the loan from party A…it creates challenges in the logistics of closing that would not be present the way other states close their transactions. For this reason, in California…Double Escrows are not preferred. Also for this reason, I and my colleagues in our closing agent roles have developed the alternative ways to close "Double Escrow" transactions. It is for this very reason that this book was written!

👍 **Benefits:** Only to party B…no use of their own funds.

👎 **Drawbacks:** Definitely not recommended. This method can be made to look very deceptive and fraudulent by attorneys for a disgruntled party A or C. In some situations and areas, double escrows may be illegal.

🎯 **Potential Uses:** *Not recommended*

16. "Subject To"

Closing a property "subject to" means purchasing a property subject to the effects of liens, loans and/or other encumbrances on the property. In a normal transaction, the liens/loans of the seller and other encumbrances like substandard conditions recorded against the title, city liens, abatements, defaults, lawsuits, etc. are cleared, removed and/or paid so that the buyer receives the property free and clear of seller's liens. In a "subject to" transaction, the buyer is accepting the property with the liens of the seller still in place.

Generally speaking this cannot be achieve with institutional financing. A bank, credit union or normal institutional lender will require all of the sellers liens and encumbrances to be cleared prior to closing the transaction. Hard money financing will work in some circumstances especially if the lien is a non-money item such as a substandard property condition lien or abatement. When purchasing with cash, there are no limitations…you can close with whatever liens/encumbrances on the property that the buyer will accept.

Often, as investors, we plan to purchase the property in its current state and we will resolve the issues with the property. This is taking the property subject-to. It is probably for that reason that the property is being sold at a discount. In fact, sometimes the seller believes they cannot sell the property until the issue is fixed. This is an opportunity for an investor to step in and obtain the property at a discount.

Real Scenario: *An agent that I work with had an REO listing that had a lawsuit on the property. The timing and nature of the lawsuit in relationship to the foreclosure were such that the lawsuit could quite easily be won by the property owner. However, the bank that owned the property put it in their "problem properties" portfolio at a deep discount and put it on the market as is. It was apparent that the bank did not want to deal with the situation or had no expertise in doing so.*

The agent found a buyer that bought it at a deep discount and then took care of the short legal battle to clear up the issues on the property. This was a windfall purchase for the buyer.

On another transaction, my client found a property that had been burned in a fire. It was a multi-unit property but only had fire damage to one unit. The owner of the property did not have insurance and didn't have the money to fix the property. Ultimately, the city "red tagged" the building and tenants moved out. The fines and city problems made it impossible for the seller to rectify the situation. It was sold as is and my client bought it "subject to" the issues on the property. He subsequently fixed up the property, rectified the city liens and abatements and realized a very profitable situation.

👍 **Benefits:** Allows for a fast close where others may think closing a transaction is not possible. Works with all the other methods of closing described here. May allow the buyer to negotiate a deeper discount because they are taking on the seller's problems.

👎 **Drawbacks:** Does not work with financial institution financing and limited use with hard money financing.

🎯 **Potential Uses:** Multiple situations. Especially when there are city abatements or substandard liens regarding the condition of the property.

17. Option Contract

An option contract is the right to buy a property in the future for some specified price. It is similar to a "Lease Option Agreement", which is a lease with the option to buy. An investor can pay the homeowner a fee for the right to buy the property in the future usually at some set price. If the investor is then going to wholesale the transaction, they sell that right (or option) to the end buyer. With a properly drawn up contract this will be perfectly legal and should be quite simple.

Note: It is a very good idea to record the option with the county recorder or courthouse. The homeowner may forget that they sold you that option and attempt to sell the property to someone else. If that occurs and your agreement was recorded, they will not be able to complete that transaction without you signing off on the sale (for a fee of course).

👍 **Benefits:** Clean, simple and legal. Usually will only require a small cash outlay by the investor but locks in the right to buy the property from the seller. Can be used to allow additional time to find an end buyer.

👎 **Drawbacks:** Make sure your option contract is properly prepared in accordance with local laws and recorded.

🎯 **Potential Uses:** This method can be used in numerous situations. Can be favorable in situations where the seller does not want to enter a sales contract yet, but the investor wants to lock them in. Also a good way to allow a long period of time to find the end buyer.

18. Installment Sale (owner financing)

An installment sale is the sale of a property over time via periodic installments or payments. It is like putting the property on layaway but owning it today. One difference to an installment sale and normal layaway is that it is normal to see the property deeded to the buyer at the closing of the sale. This provides the buyer with control to be able to start working on the property or even obtain construction financing. Installment sales were very popular back in the 1970s and prior. Now that institutional financing is so readily available this has not been a popular choice for quite some time.

👍 **Benefits:** May give the buyer ownership of the property immediately with more favorable financing than using a financial institution. Gives the buyer flexibility and control over payment and terms. Could be used to set up a residual income stream for the seller.

👎 **Drawbacks:** The property still is tied to the seller and could potentially require the seller's participation when one sells to the end user.

Potential Uses: To obtain control of the property with very minimal resources and potentially better financing. When dealing with family members or close friends.

19. Consult and/or Project Manage the Construction

There will be circumstances where the proposed seller doesn't want to sell their property, but it is in disrepair. They may wish to fix up the property themselves so that they can live in it or rent it out. Other times, the seller may want to sell but wants to obtain a much higher price. In order to do so, repairs or upgrades would have to be made to the property. You can consult on the project. You can also project manage the construction.

Many homeowners have had a bad experience with a contractor in the past. For some people, the worst part of fixing up a property is dealing with the contractors. Often, people would gladly pay someone a consulting fee or project management fee to ensure the project is completed on time or that it is done in an appropriate way.

An experienced flipper can bring much value in this method. For one, an experienced flipper may be able to bring his contractors, his work crews, his handymen, etc. Second, an experienced flipper would know how to keep the project on track, meet timelines and deadlines, maintain security of the property, etc. This experience brings much value to the homeowner. Party C may even be interested in hiring you for this work after you have wholesaled the property to them.

One flipper that I know uses this business model. He will wholesale deals to other investors and bring his contractors and crew to do the work. At times, he even brings his own hard money team. This allows Party C to just "show up" and take the deal. He makes money on the wholesale when Party C buys the property. Plus he makes a project management fee for the construction. Who knows...he probably gets a referral fee from the Hard Money Lender and the Contractor as well!

At times, the project manager is paid a flat fee or percentage of the construction costs. Others may structure the fee as a percentage of equity created. **Be sure to check your local laws to see if licenses are required for the work that you plan to do.**

👍 **Benefits:** Can help you get paid even when the seller does not sell. May mean a second check for you on deals where you have already made a wholesale fee.

👎 **Drawbacks:** This is probably best used by the experienced person who knows construction projects and how to manage them. Flippers/wholesalers that are new in the business will not likely bring much value.

🎯 **Potential Uses:** When the seller does not want to sell, but work is still required. When wholesaling to a new flipper (Party C) this service may be a huge benefit to them. ANYTIME.

20. Bonus Material

Title Insurance Binder— Guaranteed way to save up to $1,000 or more on every flip!

When someone is buying a property and plans to sell that property within 2 years, it is advisable to request a binder from the title insurance company. A binder is a contract to issue title insurance at a future date (the date the owner sells the property) in lieu of issuing a policy to that owner now. If a title matter arises that will cause a title claim, the policy owner can convert that binder into a policy at that time. Be sure to read the binder coverage and obtain legal advice.

Upon purchase, the binder costs an extra 10% of the policy price, around $100-$200 when dealing with flips at California's median price. The benefit in obtaining a binder is that at the time of the sale the seller will realize a savings of about $1,000+ (again at California's median home prices).

Title Insurance Interim Binder

In some cases, when dealing with wholesaling and flips, an investor (B) will buy a property then immediately sell it to another party (C) for a small profit (wholesale fee or skinny flip). C will perform the rehab and flip the property. When doing so, B requests a binder during the original purchase in order to save money upon the sale of the property. However, B may want to pass the binder on to C. To do so they will request an Interim Binder which costs 75% less than title insurance would and passes the binder over to C. Then C will execute the binder upon completion of the rehab and sale of the property.

Not all companies will do Interim Binders, so check with your title company.

Seller Carry Back

When money is easily available and real estate financing is flowing readily, seller carry backs are not very common. However, when financing tightens they become more prevalent. A seller carry back is where some or all of the financing for the purchase of the property is coming from the seller's equity in the form of a note or mortgage against the property. In other words, the seller is acting as the bank providing the financing for the purchase.

Many sellers like the idea of this because it allows them to receive a monthly check from the buyer (the mortgage payment). Buyers like this idea because of more flexible terms, easier qualification, and often better rates and fewer fees than would have otherwise been available. A seller carry back could be the difference in an investor's ability to close a transaction or not. This scenario will illustrate:

B orchestrated the purchase of the property for $100k with fix and flip financing for $80k. The fix and flip lender would cover the cost of the rehab so that B only had to cover the 20% down payment or $20k. B did not have enough money to make this happen. However, the seller was willing to carry a second trust deed (mortgage) because B informed them that it would increase their payout by 10% ($2k) based on the terms they negotiated. B made the deal happen because of the seller carry back.

The escrow or closing agent will typically prepare the documents required for a seller carry back.

All-Inclusive Trust Deed (AITD)

The all-inclusive trust deed is a form of a seller carry back in which the sellers financing is remaining in place.

For instance, the seller has a mortgage of $180k on the property from ABC Bank and the buyer likes the terms of that loan so they wish to keep the financing in place. They agree to a sales price of $250k for the property. The seller does not wish to sell the property subject to the loan from ABC Bank because if the buyer does not make the payments their credit will be negatively impacted.

They agree to an AITD. The seller will carry an AITD for $200k ($180k of which is the original loan from ABC Bank and $20k which the seller is carrying). The buyer is putting down the other $50k in cash. They determine the terms of the loan and the buyer is responsible for paying the payment every month. Out of that payment, the seller keeps their portion and pays the payment to ABC Bank.

The AITD takes away the normal risk in a subject to transaction of the seller's credit being messed up by the buyer not paying the mortgage to ABC Bank. The seller is still responsible for the payment. The buyer has the risk that the seller does not actually make the payment and the loan at ABC Bank goes into default. This is easily mitigated, however, by an arrangement in which the buyer makes part of the payment directly to ABC Bank and the rest to the seller or where the seller proves payment was made to ABC Bank each month before the next payment is due.

Creating Your Own List Of Cash Buyers

Do you desire a list of buyers that are ready to purchase properties with cash?

Do you struggle to find buyers that you know can close on a real property transaction in a short time period even where there are unknown risks?

Are you interested in building your list of cash buyers who are searching for deals in this market and have a proven record of purchasing with cash?

If you answered yes to any of these questions, then you have found the solution! If you go to www.KevinSayles.com and download the free report **The GUARANTEED Way Build Your Cash Buyer List Within 7 Days.**

A list of cash buyers will be an invaluable tool to your business!

Conclusion

With the information you have just read, you are now "armed and dangerous"! No matter what the situation, you will have a means to get the deal closed. I suggest that you read this book again to let the information sink in. You want this information in your arsenal. Keep this as a reference guide for your business.

You may find that for your next 10 deals you use method 5(a) every time. Then out of the clear blue sky 2 years from now, you have a deal where you cannot use 5(a). That is when you pull this book out and see which solution best fits.

You may find that each of your next 5 deals require a different solution. Pull this book out each time and apply the appropriate solution. The market may change this month and a whole new type of transaction requires gaining new knowledge and experience. This book will be your reference.

No matter what the scenario, no matter what the future holds, refer back to this guide to help you close your transactions and make money wholesaling real estate!

After writing and editing this book I realized something that I want to offer to all my readers. For a 26+ year veteran in this industry, all of the methods for closing wholesale deals make perfect sense to me and are easy to understand. I know, however, that some of my readers may be newer to this business, or may just require more detail in order to fully understand how structuring the closing will work for them. So I will be offering a very economical online course to provide detailed, exact "how-to's" of setting up these closings. You will be trained well enough to be able to instruct your closing agent and maneuver even the most difficult and challenging distressed property situations. For more info, stay tuned at www.KevinSayles.com. Oh, and yes this was a shameless plug!

If you liked this book, please go back to wherever you purchased it and write a 5-star review for us. If you require help closing a transaction, find me at www.KevinSayles.com. Thank you for reading this guide!

ABOUT THE AUTHOR

Kevin Sayles obtained a Bachelor of Science degree with departmental honors from the University of La Verne, Magna Cum Laude, and an MBA from the University of Redlands. He started his career in the real estate industry by working in banking beginning in 1993. While working for some of the nation's largest savings institutions, Kevin received extensive training in lending, sales, appraisals, escrow and title, and of course retail and commercial banking. It was there he received his introduction to both real estate closings and probate.

Kevin is a real estate investor and an expert in closing difficult transactions. Since the late 1990's, he has used his experience in the field of title insurance (real estate closing services). He has a "never say die" attitude and knows how to close the deals!

It is estimated that he has closed well over 17,000 transactions while working as a title representative. He uses his knowledge and first-hand experience to help close even the toughest transactions.

Currently, Kevin helps real estate agents and investors close transactions as a title representative and probate specialist.

www.KevinSayles.com

Kevin has more titles coming soon! Stay tuned at www.KevinSayles.com

Find his other hit book on Amazon:

www.ingramcontent.com/pod-product-compliance
Lightning Source LLC
Chambersburg PA
CBHW071227220526
45468CB00002B/764

* 9 7 8 1 7 9 2 8 8 1 3 6 7 *